D

WILD DOGS

Consultant : Ronald M. Nowak
Illustrators: Barbara Gibson, Theophilus Britt Griswold

Published by
The National Geographic Society
John M. Fahey, Jr., President and Chief Executive Officer
Gilbert M. Grosvenor, Chairman of the Board
Nina D. Hoffman, Senior Vice President
William R. Gray, Vice President and Director, Book Division

Staff for this Book
Barbara Brownell, Director of Continuities
Marianne R. Koszorus, Senior Art Director
Toni Eugene, Editor
Alexandra Littlehales, Art Director
Marfé Ferguson Delano, Writer-Researcher
Susan V. Kelly, Illustrations Editor
Sharon Kocsis Berry, Illustrations Assistant
Mark A. Caraluzzi, Director of Direct Response Marketing
Heidi Vincent, Product Manager
Vincent P. Ryan, Manufacturing Manager
Lewis R. Bassford, Production Project Manager

Visit our Web site at www.nationalgeographic.com

Library of Congress Catalog Card Number: 99-70470
ISBN: 0-7922-3456-1

Color separations by Quad Graphics, Martinsburg, West Virginia
Printed in Mexico by R.R. Donnelley & Sons Company

DOGS
AND
WILD DOGS

MARFÉ FERGUSON DELANO

All photographs supplied by Animals Animals/Earth Scenes

NATIONAL
GEOGRAPHIC
SOCIETY

INTRODUCTION

The pet, or domestic, dog has 35 wild relatives in the dog family. Wild dogs can be found almost everywhere in the world except Antarctica. They live in habitats ranging from deserts to tropical forests to frozen tundras.

Wild dogs are mainly meat-eating hunters that capture their prey by running it down or pouncing on it. Bigger dogs often work in groups to capture animals larger than themselves. Smaller dogs tend to hunt alone, preying on small mammals. They may also eat insects and fruit.

Most wild dogs have keen senses of smell, hearing, and sight, which help them find their prey. Long legs and deep chests give wild dogs the strength and speed they need to catch prey. Strong jaws and sharp teeth help them hold and kill it.

Wild dogs live in family groups or alone. They communicate through scent, facial expressions, body posture, and sound. Some wild dogs mate for life. Both parents help care for the young.

Many wild dogs today are quite rare due to hunting by humans and the taking over of their habitats by people.

HOW TO USE THIS BOOK

The dogs in this book are organized in two sections. In the first section you will meet 20 wild dogs. The second features 14 domestic dogs. Both sections are arranged from heaviest to smallest dog. Each spread helps you identify one kind of dog and tells you about its size, color, and behavior. For each wild dog, a map tells where it lives. For each domestic dog, a map shows where it came from. The "Field Notes" entry gives an interesting fact about the dog. If you find a word you do not know, look it up in the Glossary on page 76.

GRAY WOLF

 The gray wolf is the largest wild dog. It lives in packs of five to eight dogs. Led by the strongest male and his mate, pack members work together to hunt, defend territory, and raise pups.

WHERE TO FIND:

NORTH AMERICA EUROPE ASIA

Gray wolves live in forests, tundra, swamps, and prairies in parts of North America, Europe, and Asia.

WHAT TO LOOK FOR:

✳ **SIZE**
Gray wolves vary in length from 4 to 6½ feet, including the tail.

✳ **COLOR**
A gray wolf's fur can be white, gray, brown, sandy yellow, or black.

✳ **BEHAVIOR**
Wolves team up to bring down big game such as moose and deer.

✳ **MORE**
An adult wolf may eat almost 20 pounds of meat in one meal.

FIELD NOTES

Wolves usually hunt in packs, but sometimes catch smaller prey, such as fish, on their own.

Large, pointed ears help a gray wolf hear other wolves howling more than six miles away.

RED WOLF

 Primarily night hunters, red wolves feed mainly on rabbits, rodents, raccoons, and deer. These wolves make dens in hollow tree trunks or dig burrows in stream banks or sandy hills in coastal areas.

WHERE TO FIND:

UNITED STATES

Red wolves once roamed the southeastern U.S. but now live in the wild only in a North Carolina refuge.

WHAT TO LOOK FOR:

✳ SIZE
A red wolf measures over 5 feet long, including the tail, and weighs between 45 and 90 pounds.

✳ COLOR
Its fur is usually cinnamon or tan.

✳ BEHAVIOR
Red wolves live in small packs of a mated pair and their pups.

✳ MORE
Loss of habitat and hunting by humans have made this wolf nearly extinct.

The red wolf has longer ears and a narrower muzzle than its cousin the gray wolf.

AFRICAN WILD DOG

Living in large family packs, the African wild dog is the most social, or cooperative, of all dogs. Food from a kill is shared with any pack member that is hungry, including pups and injured animals.

Pups are born in litters of 6 to 16. At about three months of age, they join in the hunt for the first time. By nine months, they can kill easy prey.

WHERE TO FIND:
African wild dogs live in scattered packs of 10 to 20 dogs in grasslands, savannas, and open woodlands.

WHAT TO LOOK FOR:

✷ SIZE
They stand up to 30 inches tall at the shoulder and weigh 37 to 79 pounds.

✷ COLOR
Their short fur is a patchwork of black, tan, yellow, and white.

✷ BEHAVIOR
Only the highest-ranking male and female in a pack produce offspring.

✷ MORE
African wild dogs usually hunt in the morning and early evening.

MANED WOLF

 Named for the mane of coarse black fur on the back of its neck, this rare, shaggy-coated wild dog is a wolf in name only. Unlike most true wolves, the maned wolf lives alone except during breeding time.

WHERE TO FIND:
The maned wolf can be found in grasslands and swampy regions of central South America.

SOUTH AMERICA

WHAT TO LOOK FOR:

✳ **SIZE**
It may reach nearly 3 feet at the shoulder and weigh up to 50 pounds.

✳ **COLOR**
The maned wolf's coat is golden red, with a black mane and black legs.

✳ **BEHAVIOR**
Maned wolves are active at dusk and at night.

✳ **MORE**
They eat fruit, insects, birds, and small mammals they can catch alone.

The maned wolf raises both legs on one side of its body as it walks, which gives it a distinctive gait.

The maned wolf's extra-long legs give it a good view of prey hiding in tall grass.

DHOLE

 Dholes (DOLZ) are clever hunters that prey on deer, wild sheep, and antelopes. To capture prey, dholes often separate an animal from its herd. Then the pack surrounds the prey to bring it down.

WHERE TO FIND:
The dhole, rare throughout its range, inhabits forests, mountainous regions, plains, and jungles in Asia.

WHAT TO LOOK FOR:

✳ SIZE
A dhole measures up to 5 feet long, including its tail, and weighs between 22 and 46 pounds.

✳ COLOR
It is rusty red, with a black-tipped tail.

✳ BEHAVIOR
Dholes often use whistling sounds to communicate over long distances.

✳ MORE
A pack of dholes will sometimes drive a tiger, bear, or leopard from its kill.

The dhole's distinctive coloring lends it the common name, the red dog.

DINGO

 Dingoes live as wild dogs today, but scientists believe they started out as partly tamed dogs that traveled with sailors to Australia more than 3,500 years ago. On arrival, they escaped and ran wild.

WHERE TO FIND:
Dingoes inhabit dense forests, open plains, and deserts in Australia and are also found in New Guinea.

AUSTRALIA

WHAT TO LOOK FOR:

✳ SIZE
Dingoes are about six feet long, including the tail.

✳ COLOR
Most dingoes have yellowish fur. Some are white, black, brown, or reddish.

✳ BEHAVIOR
Dingoes hunt alone or in groups, depending on the size of their prey.

✳ MORE
Females give birth to a litter of four or five pups each year.

Dingoes resemble medium-size pet dogs but have a longer muzzle.

FIELD NOTES

Tireless hunters, dingoes often work in pairs to bring down large prey such as kangaroos.

COYOTE

 Coyotes will eat almost anything—rabbits and mice, fish and frogs, snakes and lizards, nuts and fruit. The variety of their diet helps coyotes adapt to a variety of habitats. Some even live in cities.

WHERE TO FIND:

NORTH AMERICA

Coyotes are at home in forests, prairies, deserts, and mountains throughout North and Central America.

WHAT TO LOOK FOR:

✳ SIZE
Coyotes stand nearly 2 feet tall at the shoulder and weigh 20 to 40 pounds.

✳ COLOR
They are shades of tan, gray, and rusty brown, with a black-tipped tail.

✳ BEHAVIOR
Coyotes live alone, in mated pairs, or in small family groups.

✳ MORE
People sometimes hunt coyotes because they kill lambs and calves.

Like many wild dogs, the coyote howls to state its location and to mark its territory.

GOLDEN JACKAL

 Like coyotes, golden jackals are flexible eaters. Their diet includes young gazelles—which they team up to hunt—rodents, hares, reptiles, insects, and fruit. All jackals also eat carrion, the meat of dead animals.

WHERE TO FIND:
Golden jackals inhabit dry, open country in northern Africa, southern Asia, and southeastern Europe.

EUROPE
ASIA
AFRICA

WHAT TO LOOK FOR:

✳ SIZE
Golden jackals are 15 to 19 inches tall.

✳ COLOR
Their fur runs from golden yellow to yellowish gray.

✳ BEHAVIOR
Golden jackals often stay with the same mate for life.

✳ MORE
Like many dogs, golden jackals mark their territory with urine to warn away intruders.

Bristling fur and laid back ears signal aggression in these golden jackals as well as in other dogs.

SIDE-STRIPED JACKAL

 Side-striped jackals are shy forest dwellers that usually live in small family groups. In areas where humans live nearby, these wild dogs are active only at night.

WHERE TO FIND:

The side-striped jackal lives south of Africa's Sahara. It prefers thick forests and swampy areas.

AFRICA

WHAT TO LOOK FOR:

✱ SIZE
The side-striped jackal stands about 20 inches tall at the shoulder.

✱ COLOR
Its coat is mostly grayish tan, with whitish underparts.

✱ BEHAVIOR
Side-striped jackals yap, yelp, and bark. They do not howl as other jackals do.

✱ MORE
Side-striped jackals eat fruits and vegetables as well as small animals.

This jackal is named for the stripes of white and black hairs that run along each side of its body.

Aggressive

Friendly

BLACK-BACKED JACKAL

Black-backed jackals usually make their dens in abandoned aardvark holes or in old termite mounds. They prefer to live in brushy woodlands or dry grasslands.

FIELD NOTES

Black-backed jackals often gather around a lion's kill to gobble up leftover scraps of meat.

The saddle of black-and-white fur that runs down its back gives the black-backed jackal its name.

WHERE TO FIND:

The black-backed jackal is commonly found in open country in eastern and southern Africa.

WHAT TO LOOK FOR:

✳ SIZE
The black-backed jackal is about three to four feet long, including its tail.

✳ COLOR
It is mostly reddish tan, with dark markings and a cream-colored belly

✳ BEHAVIOR
To communicate, black-backed jackals whine, growl, bark, cackle, and howl.

✳ MORE
In coastal areas, black-backed jackals eat baby seals, fish, and seabirds.

RACCOON DOG

With its short legs and masked face, this wild dog looks a lot like a real raccoon. Like its namesake, the raccoon dog usually searches at night for food. It eats small mammals, frogs, fish, insects, and fruit.

WHERE TO FIND:

The raccoon dog was once found only in Asia. It now lives in Europe, too. It was introduced there by humans.

WHAT TO LOOK FOR:

✳ SIZE
Raccoon dogs grow up to 3 feet long, including the tail. They weigh 12 to 22 pounds.

✳ COLOR
They are mainly yellowish brown.

✳ BEHAVIOR
Raccoon dogs usually hunt alone but often curl up together to rest or sleep.

✳ MORE
Raccoon dogs growl, whine, and whimper. They do not bark.

The raccoon dog usually lives in a forest, like this, or in bushy areas along lakes and streams.

FIELD NOTES
The only dog that hibernates, or rests through the winter, the raccoon dog beds down in a moss-lined burrow.

BUSH DOG

 Webbed paws help make bush dogs excellent swimmers. If prey tries to escape by jumping into water, a bush dog dives right in after it. Bush dogs live and hunt in packs of up to ten animals.

WHERE TO FIND:

Bush dogs roam grassy swamps, forests, and riverbanks from Central through South America.

WHAT TO LOOK FOR:

✷ **SIZE**
Bush dogs stand just under 12 inches tall and weigh 11 to 15 pounds.

✷ **COLOR**
Their fur is dark brown.

✷ **BEHAVIOR**
They prey mainly on large rodents such as capybaras, but may also hunt deer.

✷ **MORE**
To stay in contact with each other in thick forest growth, bush dogs often make high-pitched squeaking sounds.

With its short, stocky body, the bush dog looks somewhat like a miniature bear.

FIELD NOTES

Bush dogs often drive prey—here a capybara—into the water, where hunting partners wait to ambush it.

29

RED FOX

Red foxes pounce on mice and chase down rabbits. Sometimes these night hunters dig holes and bury extra prey so that they can eat it later. Unlike wolves, foxes tend to live alone.

FIELD NOTES

To find mice, the red fox stands straight and still on its hind legs while it listens and watches.

The red fox's bushy tail is tipped with white or black. Its lower legs are usually black.

NORTH AMERICA   EUROPE   ASIA   AFRICA   AUSTRALIA

WHERE TO FIND:

The red fox lives across the northern half of the globe. It is also found in Australia; people introduced it there.

WHAT TO LOOK FOR:

✳ SIZE
Red foxes stand 12 to 16 inches tall at the shoulder.

✳ COLOR
Their fur ranges from pale yellowish red to deep reddish brown.

✳ BEHAVIOR
Red foxes care for their pups until they are about six months old.

✳ MORE
In the fall, red foxes often feed largely on berries and fruits.

GRAY FOX

 The gray fox is the only dog that can easily climb trees. It often scrambles straight up a trunk to escape a coyote or other enemy. Like a squirrel, this fox can leap gracefully from branch to branch.

WHERE TO FIND:

NORTH AMERICA

SOUTH AMERICA

The gray fox's range includes wooded and brushy areas from North into South America.

WHAT TO LOOK FOR:

✳ SIZE
The gray fox is usually about three feet long, including a one-foot tail.

✳ COLOR
It is mostly gray, with rust-colored sides and white underparts.

✳ BEHAVIOR
To communicate, gray foxes mew, growl, snarl, bark, and scream.

✳ MORE
They sometimes make dens high above the ground in hollow tree trunks.

The gray fox usually stays hidden during the day and hunts for food at dusk.

CAPE FOX

The Cape fox gets its name from its range, which extends to the Cape of Good Hope at the southern tip of Africa. Cape foxes eat mostly insects, small animals, and plants.

FIELD NOTES

When the sun goes down, the Cape fox leaves its rocky den to begin its nightly hunt for food.

A Cape fox pup greets its father. Father foxes bring food back to the den to help feed their young.

WHERE TO FIND:

AFRICA

The Cape fox inhabits dry plains and savannas in southern Africa. This fox never lives in forests.

WHAT TO LOOK FOR:

✳ SIZE
Cape foxes weigh about nine pounds and are about a foot tall at the shoulder.

✳ COLOR
Their soft, short fur is silvery gray with sandy-colored sides and legs.

✳ BEHAVIOR
To communicate, this fox lets loose a yell followed by several yaps.

✳ MORE
People hunt this fox in the mistaken belief that it preys on sheep.

CORSAC FOX

 Corsac foxes are friendlier with each other than most foxes, which tend to live alone except during the breeding season. Corsac foxes often share the same burrow. In winter they may hunt in packs.

WHERE TO FIND:

EUROPE
ASIA

The corsac fox is distributed throughout the treeless plains, or steppes, in eastern Europe and central Asia.

WHAT TO LOOK FOR:

❋ SIZE
The corsac fox measures up to three feet long, including its tail.

❋ COLOR
It is yellowish gray or silvery gray.

❋ BEHAVIOR
Corsac foxes sometimes migrate south when winter snow and ice make finding food difficult.

❋ MORE
This fox preys on mice and hares, birds and eggs, lizards and frogs.

In summer the corsac fox's coat is short and coarse, like this. In winter it is much softer and thicker.

FIELD NOTES

So easily tamed is the corsac fox that in 18th-century Russia it was often kept as a pet.

ARCTIC FOX

 A heavy fur coat keeps the arctic fox warm even at temperatures of minus 50°F. Unlike most foxes, the arctic fox has short, rounded ears, which allow very little body heat to escape through them.

NORTH AMERICA EUROPE ASIA

WHERE TO FIND:
The arctic fox lives in the tundra and coastal areas of the far north, including Iceland and Greenland.

WHAT TO LOOK FOR:

✳ **SIZE**
The arctic fox grows about three feet long, including its tail.

✳ **COLOR**
Snow white in winter, its fur turns brown or gray in summer.

✳ **BEHAVIOR**
During blizzards arctic foxes dig burrows in the snow for shelter.

✳ **MORE**
Humans sometimes hunt these foxes for their beautiful fur.

FIELD NOTES
An arctic fox may follow a polar bear onto floating ice to steal leftovers from the bear's kill.

Born in spring or summer, arctic fox pups have soft brown coats that turn thick and white before winter arrives.

BAT-EARED FOX

To avoid being carried off by birds of prey, the bat-eared fox usually hunts at night. The fox relies on its big ears, which can pick up insects moving underground, to track down its main food.

FIELD NOTES

When a bat-eared fox locates a termite nest, it digs in, devouring the insects by the mouthful.

WHERE TO FIND:

AFRICA

The bat-eared fox inhabits dry grasslands, savannas, and brushlands in eastern and southern Africa.

WHAT TO LOOK FOR:

✷ SIZE
These foxes stand about 12 inches tall.

✷ COLOR
Yellowish gray, they have black ears and a black-tipped tail.

✷ BEHAVIOR
Bat-eared foxes generally live in family groups of two to five. They often groom each other after feeding.

✷ MORE
They communicate with soft whistles and by moving their ears and tails.

Large ears allow body heat to escape, which helps the bat-eared fox stay cool in hot weather.

41

SWIFT FOX

These fast-running little foxes sleep by day in underground dens nestled as much as five feet below the earth's surface. A den may have several tunnel-like entrances, which can be 11 feet long.

FIELD NOTES

To confuse and escape a coyote or other enemy, the swift fox often runs in a zigzag pattern.

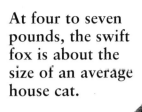

At four to seven pounds, the swift fox is about the size of an average house cat.

NORTH AMERICA

WHERE TO FIND:
The swift fox can be found on grassy plains in the central and western parts of North America.

WHAT TO LOOK FOR:

✳ SIZE
Including its bushy tail, the swift fox grows just under three feet long.

✳ COLOR
Its fur is mostly gray and rusty brown, with paler underparts.

✳ BEHAVIOR
By night the swift fox hunts mice, rabbits, and other small mammals.

✳ MORE
Swift foxes live in social groups of a mated pair and their young.

FENNEC

 Weighing in at just three pounds, the desert-dwelling fennec is the smallest wild dog. This tiny fox, which feeds on plant roots and small animals, can survive for long periods without drinking water.

WHERE TO FIND:

AFRICA

The fennec inhabits the hot, sandy deserts that stretch across northern Africa.

WHAT TO LOOK FOR:

✳ SIZE
It stands about eight inches tall at the shoulder. Its ears are six inches long.

✳ COLOR
Fennecs are light tan or cream colored.

✳ BEHAVIOR
They live in family groups of up to ten. They spend the day in dens dug in sand dunes and forage for food at night.

✳ MORE
Fennecs often play together but sometimes fight over food.

Like the bat-eared fox, the fennec has huge ears that help keep it cool in desert heat.

FIELD NOTES

The fennec has thickly furred footpads, which help it run in loose desert sand without sinking in.

DOMESTIC DOGS

From the huge Irish wolfhound to the tiny chihuahua, all domestic dogs are descended from wolves. Scientists believe that people and wolves first got together more than 12,000 years ago. Early people may have tamed wolves that prowled around campsites for leftover scraps of food. Or perhaps people raised orphaned wolf pups to work as guard dogs and hunting companions.

Over time, people began to supervise the mating of these partly-tamed dogs to produce dogs for specific purposes. For example, if a person wanted a good watchdog, he would mate two dogs with strong protective instincts. Dogs were also bred for size, color, shape, and personality.

This so-called selective breeding eventually led to the hundreds of different domestic dog breeds that exist throughout the world today. A shaded map in every entry shows where each type of domestic dog was first bred. The American Kennel Club organizes purebred dogs—those whose parents are the same breed—into the following seven groups:

Sporting dogs were first bred to track and fetch game. Working dogs pulled carts or sleds and guarded people and property. Herding dogs rounded up and protected livestock. Hounds were raised to chase game. Terriers were bred to hunt and kill rats and other small animals. Toy dogs are the smallest breeds. Nonsporting dogs include a wide range of breeds that serve primarily as pets.

Most domestic dogs are not purebred. Dogs that are a mix of two pure breeds are called crossbreeds. And dogs that blend several different breeds, like the pooch here, are called mutts.

Domestic dogs are still like wolves in many ways. They mark and defend their territories and communicate with a variety of sounds and physical signals.

IRISH WOLFHOUND

 Tallest dog in the world, the Irish wolfhound is a sight hound—that is a dog that uses its keen eyesight to locate prey and chase it down. This gentle giant needs plenty of outdoor space to explore.

WHERE IT CAME FROM:
The Irish wolfhound is an ancient breed that lived in Ireland as early as the fourth century A.D.

IRELAND

WHAT TO LOOK FOR:

✳ SIZE
The Irish wolfhound stands almost three feet tall at the shoulder.

✳ COLOR
The dog's rough, wiry coat can be gray, tan, white, sandy red, or black.

✳ BEHAVIOR
It is a calm and friendly dog that enjoys the company of people.

✳ MORE
Irish wolfhounds have shaggy fur above their eyes and on their chins.

The Irish wolfhound's long, powerful legs help it run fast and far.

FIELD NOTES

As its name suggests, the Irish wolfhound was originally used by humans for hunting wolves.

SAINT BERNARD

 No dog weighs more than the Saint Bernard, which can reach 200 pounds. A working breed, it was first used to pull carts, but it is most famous for rescuing travelers lost in the snow of the Swiss Alps.

WHERE IT CAME FROM:

SWITZERLAND

The Saint Bernard was bred in Switzerland from a dog brought there by Romans 2,000 years ago.

WHAT TO LOOK FOR:

✳ **SIZE**
These dogs are more than two feet tall.

✳ **COLOR**
They are generally white and red or red and brownish yellow.

✳ **BEHAVIOR**
The Saint Bernard is a gentle, intelligent dog that is easily trained.

✳ **MORE**
It is named for a shelter for travelers in the Swiss Alps. Monks there once used the dogs for rescue work.

The Saint Bernard's strong neck and muscular shoulders made it well suited for pulling carts.

GERMAN SHEPHERD DOG

 Few dogs perform as many jobs as the German shepherd. Bred as a herding dog, it works worldwide as a police dog, a search-and-rescue dog, and a watchdog.

WHERE IT CAME FROM:
First recognized as a breed in the 1800s, the German shepherd dog was developed in Germany.

GERMANY

WHAT TO LOOK FOR:

✳ SIZE
The German shepherd stands about two feet tall at the shoulder.

✳ COLOR
It can be black and tan, black and gray, or solid black.

✳ BEHAVIOR
It is a loyal, sensitive, highly intelligent dog that forms a strong bond with its human family.

✳ MORE
Strong hind legs make it a good jumper.

The German shepherd's erect, pointed ears and long muzzle resemble those of the wolf.

LABRADOR RETRIEVER

 True to its name, the Labrador retriever loves to fetch, or retrieve, things. Classified as a sporting dog, the Lab is used by hunters to bring in game.

WHERE IT CAME FROM:
A popular family dog, the Labrador retriever comes from Newfoundland, an island in eastern Canada.

NEWFOUNDLAND

WHAT TO LOOK FOR:

✳ **SIZE**
Labrador retrievers stand about 2 feet tall at the shoulder and weigh 55 to 80 pounds or more.

✳ **COLOR**
They are yellow or cream colored, black, or chocolate brown.

✳ **BEHAVIOR**
Labs are outgoing and affectionate and love to meet new people.

✳ **MORE**
They are often used as guide dogs.

The water-loving Labrador retriever uses its strong, paddle-like tail to steer when it swims. Its smooth, thick coat sheds water.

Fishermen in eastern Canada once used Labradors to help pull their filled nets to shore.

GREYHOUND

 With their long legs and streamlined bodies, greyhounds are running machines. When they dash at full speed, all four feet leave the ground at once. Racing dogs have been clocked at 42 miles an hour.

WHERE IT CAME FROM:
Originally from Egypt, these sleek hounds were brought to Great Britain more than 1,000 years ago.

EGYPT

WHAT TO LOOK FOR:

✳ SIZE
Greyhounds weigh 60 to 70 pounds and stand 30 inches tall at the shoulder.

✳ COLOR
They come in a variety of colors, including black, white, tan, gray, and red. Colors may be mixed.

✳ BEHAVIOR
Greyhounds have a strong instinct to chase anything that moves.

✳ MORE
Greyhounds have excellent eyesight.

Roly-poly greyhound puppies will reach their full size at about one year of age.

OLD ENGLISH SHEEPDOG

 The Old English sheepdog is well suited to outdoor life. Its thick, shaggy coat, which often hides its eyes and ears, protects it against heat, cold, and dampness.

WHERE IT CAME FROM:
Old English sheepdogs are herding dogs that were developed in Great Britain about 200 years ago.

GREAT BRITAIN

WHAT TO LOOK FOR:

✳ **SIZE**
Old English sheepdogs stand nearly two feet tall at the shoulder.

✳ **COLOR**
They are generally gray or blue-gray with white markings.

✳ **BEHAVIOR**
Without a flock to protect, this dog may try to herd the kids in the family.

✳ **MORE**
Its loud, ringing bark warns strangers to keep away from its flock.

Like a bear, an old English sheepdog shuffles when it walks but runs swiftly and gracefully.

POINTER

A sporting dog, the pointer's sharp eyesight and sensitive nose help it locate game. At the first sight of prey, the dog freezes in place, raises one foreleg, and points with its nose toward the target.

FIELD NOTES

So strong is the pointer's instinct to point out game that it starts practicing as a young puppy.

A graceful, athletic dog, the pointer has a wide chest and a long, sloping neck.

WHERE IT CAME FROM:
Popular with hunters, these dogs first came into use in Great Britain, Spain, and Germany in the 1600s.

WHAT TO LOOK FOR:

✳ SIZE
Pointers measure 2 feet or more at the shoulder and weigh up to 75 pounds.

✳ COLOR
They can be white with black or reddish brown patches, or solid colors.

✳ BEHAVIOR
Pointers are energetic dogs that need a lot of exercise to be happy and healthy.

✳ MORE
Pointers are used to hunt pheasants, quail, ducks, rabbits, and raccoons.

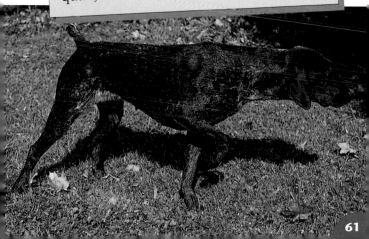

CHOW CHOW

For many centuries the chow chow—or chow for short—was used in China for hunting, herding, pulling carts, and as a guard dog. Today, this nonsporting breed serves mainly as a companion to its owner.

Its small, rounded ears and thick, fluffy mane make the chow look like a cross between a lion and a teddy bear.

FIELD NOTES

The chow's tongue is an unusual, blue-black color. A thick ruff, or mane, of fur frames its head.

CHINA

WHERE IT CAME FROM:
Chows have lived in China for 2,000 years. They were first exported to the outside world in the 1700s.

WHAT TO LOOK FOR:

✷ SIZE
Muscular and powerful, chows stand 18 to 22 inches tall at the shoulder.

✷ COLOR
They have black, red, blue-gray, cream, or cinnamon-colored fur.

✷ BEHAVIOR
An independent-minded dog, the chow tends to be reserved with strangers.

✷ MORE
The Chinese once raised chow chows for their fur and meat.

SIBERIAN HUSKY

 Beneath the Siberian husky's outer coat is a soft, woolly undercoat. The double layer of fur protects this working dog from the cold of its polar homeland. Furry footpads help it skim across snow.

WHERE IT CAME FROM:
It was bred many centuries ago by the Chukchi people of northeast Asia, in what is now called Siberia.

SIBERIA

WHAT TO LOOK FOR:

✳ SIZE
Siberian huskies weigh 35 to 60 pounds and stand almost 2 feet tall.

✳ COLOR
Their fur can be black, gray, white, red, or mixtures of these colors.

✳ BEHAVIOR
Siberian huskies are alert, friendly dogs that rarely bark but sometimes howl.

✳ MORE
Siberian huskies can have brown or blue eyes, or one of each color.

Like this dog, many Siberian huskies have a mask-like marking on their face.

FIELD NOTES
Champion long-distance runners, Siberian huskies have been used for centuries to draw sleds over snow.

DALMATIAN

 These nonsporting dogs have worked as hunting dogs, circus performers, and, in the 1800s, as coach dogs. Coach dogs ran beside or behind horse-drawn carriages to help guard the people riding inside.

WHERE IT CAME FROM:
The Dalmatian is named for Dalmatia, an area in eastern Europe where it was bred more than 250 years ago.

DALMATIA

WHAT TO LOOK FOR:

✳ **SIZE**
Dalmatians are 22 to 24 inches tall.

✳ **COLOR**
Most Dalmatians are white with black spots, but some have liver brown spots.

✳ **BEHAVIOR**
Lively and affectionate, Dalmatians are strong-minded dogs that tend to be protective of their family and home.

✳ **MORE**
Puppies are pure white at birth. Their spots appear about two weeks later.

Black-spotted Dalmatians, like this one, have a black nose. Brown-spotted Dalmatians have brown noses.

BEAGLE

The beagle is a scent hound, which means it relies on its nose more than its eyes and ears when hunting. Loving and playful by nature, this sturdy dog has long been a favorite family pet.

Large brown eyes and soft, floppy ears are trademarks of the beagle.

GREAT
BRITAIN

WHERE IT CAME FROM:
Beagle-like dogs have been
used for hunting in Great
Britain for hundreds
of years.

WHAT TO LOOK FOR:

✳ SIZE
They are 12 to 16 inches tall at the
shoulder and average 18 to 30 pounds.

✳ COLOR
Their short, thick coats are generally
white, black, and tan.

✳ BEHAVIOR
On the chase, beagles bark excitedly in
deep, ringing tones.

✳ MORE
Beagles often have an independent streak
and may tend to roam.

JACK RUSSELL TERRIER

 Like most terriers, the Jack Russell loves to dig. It was originally bred to chase foxes, burrow down after them, and flush them from their underground dens.

WHERE IT CAME FROM: Named for the man who developed the breed in the 1800s, Jack Russells first came from England.

ENGLAND

WHAT TO LOOK FOR:

✳ SIZE
They weigh 13 to 17 pounds and are about 12 inches tall at the shoulder.

✳ COLOR
Their coarse fur is white, with black or tan markings.

✳ BEHAVIOR
Bold and energetic, Jack Russells thrive on activity and attention.

✳ MORE
These clever dogs are often trained to work in movies or television.

The Jack Russell's muscular legs enable it to jump as high as four feet straight up.

FIELD NOTES

Expert rat-hunters, Jack Russells unearth prey with tough paws designed for digging.

MALTESE

 Despite its dainty looks, the Maltese is a sturdy little toy breed. It may once have been used to catch rats. During most of its 2,000-year history, however, the Maltese has been cherished as a companion.

WHERE IT CAME FROM:
The Maltese is thought to have come from the tiny island of Malta, in the Mediterranean Sea.

MALTA

WHAT TO LOOK FOR:

❋ **SIZE**
The Maltese weighs 4 to 10 pounds and stands less than 12 inches tall.

❋ **COLOR**
It has a long, silky, pure-white coat that needs frequent brushing.

❋ **BEHAVIOR**
The Maltese is a lively, sweet-natured dog that loves to romp and play.

❋ **MORE**
Maltese puppies are born with short, fluffy coats.

Maltese owners often tie a ribbon atop their dog's head to keep its hair out of its eyes.

FIELD NOTES

Once a favorite of European royalty, the Maltese is called a "lap dog," because it fits in a person's lap.

CHIHUAHUA

 The world's smallest dog, this toy breed comes in two varieties: a short-haired dog and a long-haired dog. Pint-size watchdogs, all Chihuahuas tend to bark excitedly at the slightest noise.

MEXICO

WHERE IT CAME FROM:
The Chihuahua is believed to have developed in Mexico. It is named for the state of Chihuahua.

WHAT TO LOOK FOR:

✻ **SIZE**
Chihuahuas are six to nine inches tall.

✻ **COLOR**
They come in a variety of solid and mixed colors, including tan, cream, black, and reddish brown.

✻ **BEHAVIOR**
Chihuahuas are smart, sassy little dogs that can run quickly.

✻ **MORE**
They are sensitive to cold and shiver when chilled.

Weighing just two
to six pounds,
the Chihuahua
can easily curl up
and cuddle inside
a baseball cap.

The Chihuahua has
a round, apple-shaped
head and large,
flaring ears.

75

GLOSSARY

aardvark An African mammal with a long snout that eats ants and termites.

breed A special type of domestic animal developed by people.

burrow A hole that an animal digs in the ground for its home.

den A place where an animal lives.

forage To search for food.

grassland Open land with grass growing on it.

habitat The place where an animal or plant is normally found.

hibernate To enter an inactive, sleep-like state with lowered body temperature.

mate When an adult male and female come together to produce young.

muzzle An animal's jaws and nose.

pack A group of animals that live and hunt together.

plain A large area of treeless land.

prey An animal hunted for food.

rodent A gnawing mammal, such as a rat or squirrel, that has long, chisel-shaped teeth.

savanna A grassland in tropical regions that contains scattered trees or bushes.

swamp An area of wet land with many trees and shrubs.

territory
An area claimed and defended by an animal or a group of animals.

tundra
A flat, treeless plain in Arctic and subarctic regions.

INDEX OF
DOGS AND WILD DOGS

ABOUT THE CONSULTANT

Ronald M. Nowak worked as a mammalogist in the endangered species program of the U.S. Fish and Wildlife Service for 24 years. Dr. Nowak is the author of the fourth, fifth, and sixth editions of *Walker's Mammals of the World*. He has published some 70 papers, articles, and books of scientific and popular interest.

PHOTOGRAPHIC CREDITS

Photographs supplied by Animals Animals/Earth Scenes

front cover David Welling **back cover** Fritz Prenzel **half title** M. Hamblin **title page** Alan G. Nelson 5 Rick Edwards 7 Ken Cole 9 Jim Tuten 11 Hamman/Heldring 13 Peter Weiman 15 Anup Shah 17 Fritz Prenzel 19 Joe McDonald 21 Len Rue, Jr. 23 Arthur Gloor 25 D. Allen 27 Robert Maier 29 Leonard L.T. Rhodes 31 Brian Milne 33 Alan G. Nelson 35 OSF/Bartlett, D.&J. 36 Robert Maier 39 Johnny Johnson 41 Norbert Rosing 43 C.Dani/I.Jeske 45 Miriam Agron 47 Fritz Prenzel 49 Gerard Lacz 51 Ralph Reinhold 53 Robert Pearcy 55 Robert Maier 57 Robert Pearcy 59 Henry Ausloos 61 Ralph Reinhold 62 Gerald Lacz 65 Zig Leszczynski 67 Ralph Reinhold 68 Henry Ausloos 71 George Godfrey 73 Robert Pearcy 75 Robert Pearcy 77 Pat Crowe 79 Fritz Prenzel.